EARTHQUAKES

DISASTERS

Laura Conlon

The Rourke Corporation, Inc.
Vero Beach, Florida 32964

Edited by Sandra A. Robinson

PHOTO CREDITS
© Reidar Hahn: p. 17; permission of Anchorage Museum of History
and Art: cover, p. 4; © Brock Kent: p. 18; courtesy of U.S.
Geological Survey: title page, p. 7, 8, 10, 12 (George A. Lang
Collection), 13, 15, 21

Library of Congress Cataloging-in-Publication Data

Conlon, Laura, 1959-
    Earthquakes / by Laura Conlon.
    p. cm. — (Discovery library of disasters)
    Includes index.
    Summary: An introduction to earthquakes, describing their
causes and effects, how they are measured and studied, and
ways of protecting people during an earthquake.
    ISBN 0-86593-247-6
    1. Earthquakes—Juvenile literature. [1. Earthquakes.]
I. Title II. Series.
QE521.3.C66   1993
551.2'2—dc20   92-43124
                                                     CIP
                                                      AC

TABLE OF CONTENTS

EARTHQUAKES

An earthquake is a vibration or movement of the earth's surface. Earthquakes occur more than 1,000 times a day. Most of them are so slight, they cannot be felt. Big earthquakes are extremely powerful, and they have caused most of the world's worst natural **disasters.** These disasters have resulted in a tremendous loss of human life and property.

People used to make up stories to explain earthquakes. A Russian story tells of a giant dog that caused the earth to tremble when he scratched his fleas.

Powerful earthquakes shake and shift land

WHAT CAUSES EARTHQUAKES

Today scientists think they know what causes earthquakes. Scientists believe the earth's top layer, its **crust,** is broken up into eight to 12 huge rock plates. The plates shift and grind against one another. The pressure caused by the grinding is sometimes so great that the rock plates shift and split. This causes an earthquake.

Earthquakes can also be caused by the movement of hot melted rock, called **magma,** inside the earth.

In 1971, a quake collapsed a section of interstate highway in California

WHAT HAPPENS IN AN EARTHQUAKE

An earthquake shakes the ground. Objects fall. Windows rattle. Land begins to rise and fall. Buildings tremble and sometimes split. Cracks appear in the ground, and rivers may even change direction.

A quake may last for a few seconds, or for a few minutes. Big earthquakes are often followed by smaller **aftershocks**—shocks that shake the earth days or weeks after the major quake.

Alaska's great earthquake on March 27, 1964, wrecked houses on this hillside in Anchorage

WHAT HAPPENS AFTER AN EARTHQUAKE

Not all of the damage that follows an earthquake is the result of shock waves. The earth's movement can also cause destructive fires by breaking underground gas pipes. This happened during the San Francisco earthquake in 1906.

Underwater earthquakes can cause huge waves called **tsunamis.** Tsunamis can create terrible damage when they strike the shore.

Earthquakes can also trigger falling mud and snow—**landslides**—that can destroy whole villages.

The waterfront at Seward, Alaska, was pounded by a tsunami after the 1964 quake

*After the Tokyo-Yokohama earthquake and fire of 1923, the photographer wrote,
"Yokohama was a city of the dead"*

The great San Francisco earthquake in 1906 caused major fires and destruction

WHERE EARTHQUAKES TAKE PLACE

A **fault** is a crack in the earth's crust. The edges of the rocky plates covering the earth are large faults. Many earthquakes (and volcanoes) take place at these faults. One of these areas, called the Ring of Fire, is around the edge of the Pacific Ocean.

The famous San Andreas fault is in California. Scientists are concerned about the possibility of a major earthquake along the San Andreas fault.

Earthquakes and volcanoes (shown here) most often occur along the Pacific Ring of Fire

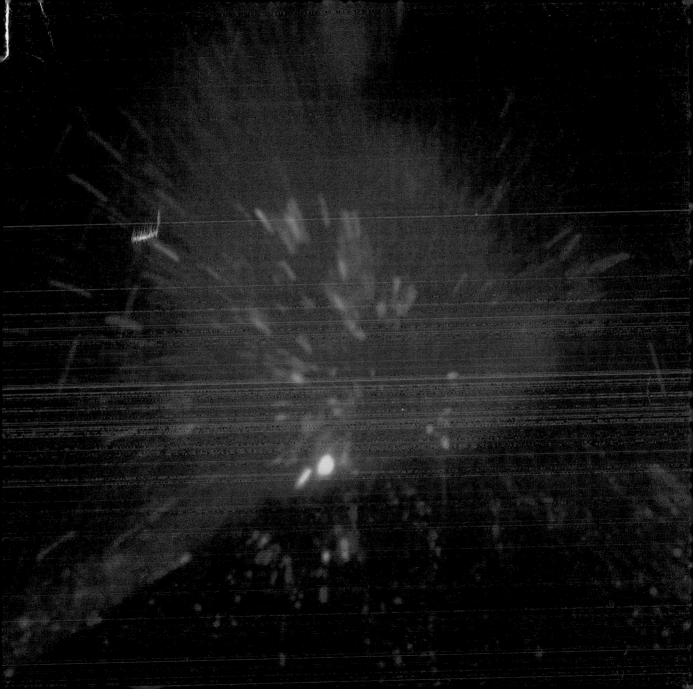

EARTHQUAKE DISASTERS

Throughout history, powerful earthquakes have caused disaster. An earthquake in 1201 may have killed over 1,000,000 people in Egypt. The 1976 Tank-shan earthquake in China killed 750,000.

The most severe earthquake in the United States happened in New Madrid, Missouri, in 1811. It caused church bells to ring as far away as Boston. It also caused the Mississippi River to flow backward for a short time.

In 1906 two large quakes shook San Francisco. The three-day fire that followed did more damage than the quakes.

16

When the ground moves, snapping wires and gas pipelines, fires often occur

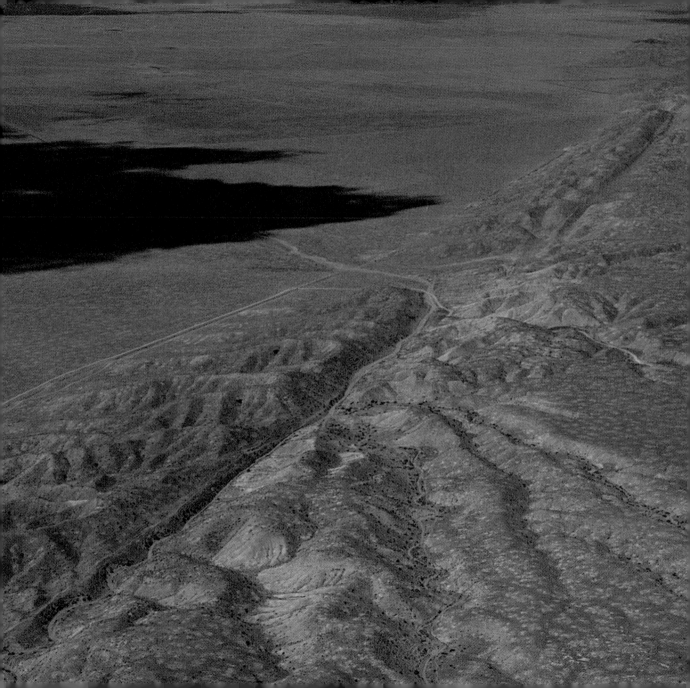

MEASURING EARTHQUAKES

Scientists use an instrument called a **seismograph** to record the strength of an earthquake. The shock waves, or tremors, are measured on a **Richter scale.** If an earthquake measures below 4 on the 9-point scale, it is usually not serious. An earthquake that measures over 7 points is usually very destructive.

An earthquake's shock waves are most powerful near the center of the quake.

Scientists study the San Andreas fault, seen from an airplane above California

STUDYING EARTHQUAKES

Using certain clues, scientists can predict some earthquakes. A seismograph can record **foreshocks**—small tremors that happen before a quake. Underground water levels are another clue—they may rise or fall before an earthquake.

Scientists hope they may someday be able to control earthquakes by pumping liquid into faults. The liquid might coat the rocks and allow them to slide gently by each other instead of grinding.

Careful construction and scientific know-how may someday reduce the risk of earthquake damage

PROTECTING PEOPLE FROM AN EARTHQUAKE

People who live where earthquakes happen should locate places of safety in case of a quake. They should store emergency supplies there, such as food, water, blankets and flashlights.

Some buildings of steel and concrete are designed to survive earthquakes. The pyramid-shaped Transamerica Building in San Francisco was built to withstand quakes.

Glossary

aftershock (AF ter shahk) — a smaller quake or series of quakes that follow the main quake

crust (KRUHST) — the outer layer of the earth

disaster (diz AS ter) — an event that causes a great loss of property and/or lives

fault (FAWLT) — a crack in the earth's crust

foreshock (FOR shahk) — a minor earthquake that happens before a larger quake

landslide (LAND slide) — falling mud, snow or rocks

magma (MAG ma) — hot melted rock under the earth's surface

Richter scale (RIHK ter SKALE) — a system for determining the strength of an earthquake

seismograph (SIZE ma graf) — an instrument used to record the direction, strength and duration of an earthquake

tsunami (soo NAH mee) — a huge wave caused by an undersea earthquake or volcano

INDEX